C000293407

The Library Called Life

By Our Betty

Collated by
Helen Pearson

**Grosvenor House
Publishing Limited**

All rights reserved
Copyright © Helen Pearson, 2022

The right of Helen Pearson to be identified as the author of this
work has been asserted in accordance with Section 78
of the Copyright, Designs and Patents Act 1988

Cover design and illustrations by Faye Needham and Helen Pearson

This book is published by
Grosvenor House Publishing Ltd
Link House
140 The Broadway, Tolworth, Surrey, KT6 7HT.
www.grosvenorhousepublishing.co.uk

This book is sold subject to the conditions that it shall not, by way of
trade or otherwise, be lent, resold, hired out or otherwise circulated
without the author's or publisher's prior consent in any form of binding or
cover other than that in which it is published and
without a similar condition including this condition being imposed
on the subsequent purchaser.

A CIP record for this book
is available from the British Library

ISBN 978-1-80381-157-4

In loving memory of My Mum

Introduction

Mum enjoyed expressing herself in writing – mainly poems but some hymns and articles for local magazines. Her love of nature and her religious beliefs are evident in many of these writings but, as a friend (who is not religious) said recently, "Without them appearing too religious – more spiritual." Several of these were written during very difficult times – the Second World War and rationing, for example.

I have chosen some of her writings to put in this book, which I hope you will enjoy. Where I know about any previous publication details then these are included. Some of her works however have not, to my knowledge, been previously published.

Many thanks go to my husband, Trevor Pearson, and my good friends, Sally Bly and Faye Needham, for all their help, support and encouragement with putting this book together. You are all so very special to me.

In 1953, Mum wrote:

> I have found the secret of happiness in the consideration of the great pattern of life, in which each one of us has the privilege to share. I have stopped asking about the purpose of it all – the beginning and the end of it. No-one knows! I am content to live, to marvel at the beauty of the earth; to admire and appreciate the work which man has done in the world through the ages. The creation of music and art, or jet planes or television. I am content to give my share to this great pattern, be it great or small, as fate decrees. I will accept anything which life brings, be it joy or pain.

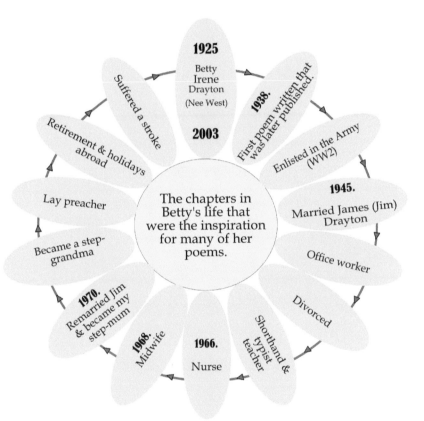

Betty's Library of Life

1925
Betty
Irene
Drayton
(Nee West)

2003

Suffered a stroke

1938.
First poem written that
was later published.

Retirement & holidays
abroad

Enlisted in the Army
(WW2)

Lay preacher

1945.
Married James (Jim)
Drayton

Became a step-
grandma

Office worker

The chapters in
Betty's life that
were the inspiration
for many of her
poems.

1970.
Remarried Jim
& became my
step-mum

Divorced

1968.
Midwife

1966.
Nurse

Shorthand &
typist
teacher

My Step Mum (hereafter referred to as Mum), Betty Irene West, was born on 25th May 1925 in the Lincolnshire village of North Somercotes.

A couple of years later her only sibling, a brother, Frederick Stanley West was born (known to family, friends and locals as "Stan"). Both loved village life.

Mum and Uncle Stan

North Somercotes
15th June 1930

It was a proud boast of Mum's that the only school she ever attended was a Church of England village school. All the teachers at that time were practising Christians, so she gained a rich religious education.

'Heaven' was written by Mum in 1938, when she was 13, and published in the Louth Standard, Louth Advertiser and Methodist Recorder in that year. I think that it may have been the first poem she wrote that was published.

It was also later published on 19th February, 1955, in the New Zealand Methodist Times – well before the World Wide Web was available to the public! In a letter from the Editor, Rev. W. T. Blight, dated 3rd August, 1955, it states "I do not know how I came by the poem 'Heaven' but I thought it beautiful; so I put it in the 'Times' …Our paper has a circulation of 5,000, which is quite good for us: we are not a very large church: 27,000 members in all New Zealand…"

"This poem was composed by a young schoolgirl, Betty West, a fourteen-year-old scholar at North Somercotes School. The headmaster states the children were told to compose a poem and Betty wrote 'Heaven' inside of thirty minutes." *The New Zealand Methodist Times, 19th February, 1955, page 659 – A Child's Poem On Heaven.*

Heaven

Oh! What is Heaven?
The sunset on yon hill,
The silence in yon church, so still,
The beauty of yon tree,
The roaring of yon deep, blue sea;
Oh! This is Heaven!

Oh! What is Heaven?
The twinkling of yon star,
As it shines from the deep, dark sky so far,
The children's pattering feet,
The singing of the birds so sweet;
Oh! This is Heaven!

Oh! What is Heaven?
The cawing of that black rook,
The music of the rippling brook,
The heather'd rocky moors,
All green nature out of doors;
Oh! This is Heaven!

Oh! What is Heaven?
Yon field of daisies bright,
Yon graceful long-necked swan so white,
That shining rainbow's glow,
All wondrous nature here below;
Oh! This is Heaven!

*Mum met my Dad,
James Robert Drayton
(Jim), a couple of
years before he was
enlisted into the army
for World War II. Dad
wasn't much of a
letter writer, but he
sent her photos.*

*She wrote to and
about him, here is one
example.*

A Gift to Jim (in Egypt) (June, 1943)

From a window looking over woodland cool,
Like a patchwork quilt, with the mingled colours
Of each tree.
And in the hollow a shallow pool,
Where seagulls bathe their snowy feathers.
Oh! That you could see!
That you could feel this still.
The clouds that gently stir among the deepest blue.
That I could put this peace and beauty in a picture,
And send it all, my love to you.

Mum and her brother, Stan, both enlisted in World War II. Stan, bein
younger than Mum, was not involved until 1945. She told me that s
did quite a bit of army training at Whip-Ma-Whop-Ma-Gate in York.

Mum told a lie to get
enlisted early in the war
efforts saying that she was
born in 1924 instead of
1925! Her army book
proves this.

They wrote about each other in 1943 – they both had such a good sense of humour.

Our Betty

Our Betty's in the A.T.S.
    Her job is spotting Jerries,
Now she's an able instructress,
    And gives old Hitler worries.

She spots by day, she spots by night,
    For Huns that do not come,
Until her golden hair goes white,
    And her fingers go all numb.

She's on an Anti-aircraft gun,
    You know, what goes off... POP!
And all the girls then start to run,
    And duck their heads or drop.

She lectures to a giggly mob
    Of spotters lean and lanky,
And my word she has a job,
    And don't she put it swanky.

But still our Betty likes the job,
    Her spirit's not diminished,
And old Hitler'd best look out,
    The war will soon be finished.

Our Stan

My brother is a clerk,
   In an office spic and span,
And now that he has learned to type,
   He thinks that he's a man.

He soon wears out his trousers seat,
   With sitting all day long,
He thinks that sitting tapping keys,
   Makes his muscles strong.

Tap, tap, tap, all through the day,
   Letters A, B, C and D,
But I would rather stand and talk
   About the ME 323.

Sitting by an office fire,
   While I stand cold and numb,
But never mind, I'll get the laugh,
   When the Hun decides to come.

Keep on tapping little boy,
   While I stand and freeze,
Otherwise perhaps you'll type,
   "This way to Heaven please".

We are still in 1943. The poem opposite may have been written after the bombing of Louth Malt Kiln that year but I am unsure.

Mum wrote, "We were afraid the church would be bombed. The spire was often so clearly visible."

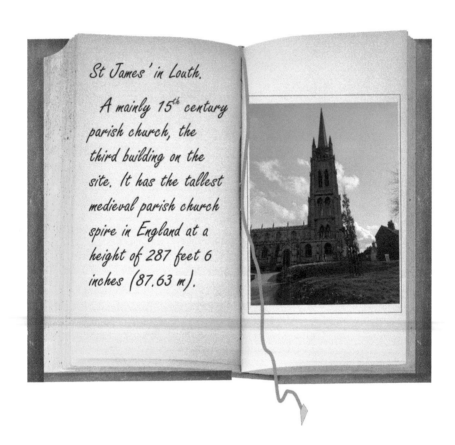

St James' in Louth.

A mainly 15th century parish church, the third building on the site. It has the tallest medieval parish church spire in England at a height of 287 feet 6 inches (87.63 m).

St James' Louth

You're my inspiration, steeple,
    Rising, tall and grey,
As I see you, slender, graceful,
    Greeting each new day.

When I look my eyes go upward,
    To the heights they soar,
Mind and soul both flying heavenward,
    Reaching Heaven's door.

In my mind I take a portrait,
    Fresh as days go by,
That takes my thoughts from hate and war,
    And up to God on high.

I believe that this poem was written in Spring, 1944, whilst Mum was serving in World War II – she is obviously missing her home.

It was published in Louth Canners' Magazine, No 1 in the early 1950s, and in Lincolnshire Life, Vol 1, No 2, Summer, 1961, page 42 – Poetry Corner. It was also accepted for publication in The Lincolnshire Poacher in November 1955 but the publication of this magazine was ceased in early 1956, before the poem could be included.

Lincolnshire

County of marshes, fens and drains,
    My thoughts are with you,
        Now Spring's green fingers touch your lanes,
        And young buds burst through.
           Violets 'neath your hedgerows,
           Gulls calls overhead,
                Rippling streams where willow grows,
                Paths I yearn to tread.

That I might walk where dykes are lined,
    With king cups' golden mass,
        And cowslips and cuckoo flowers find,
        Among the waving grass.
           To hear the church bells echo clear,
           O'er acres flat and wide,
                To see tall spires and towers appear,
                Across the countryside.

I'll walk your sandy shores once more,
    And smell the strong salt air.
        I'll hear the North Sea rage and roar,
        To you I can compare
           No other place, where'ere I go,
           In countries far or near,
                And I'll come home some day I know,
                To my dear Lincolnshire.

In 1944 Mum wrote about one of her fellow plane spotters!

Olive

A girl called Olive stood and spotted,
Spotted till her legs were rotted,
Till now they ache with all the strain,
Refuse to hold her up again.

So when you see poor Olive limp,
Like a weary land-bound shrimp,
Remember 'twas for you she spotted,
Don't laugh because her legs are rotted.

On 18th November, 1945 Mum wrote:

My Pen

What fascination has my pen,
And what delight I find,
To put on paper all the thoughts
Which linger in my mind.

To write loving words of comfort,
To him that is my friend,
To write a verse on this and that,
To make my ideas blend.

But may I ever remember,
To write my words with care,
And leave the cruel words that hurt,
Just bring happiness there.

Mum wrote about Stan going away in 1945, obviously very concerned about him – her little brother. He was in Ceylon in 1945/1946.

To my Brother (18th November, 1945)

He goes away with the light of adventure in his eyes,
A young boy, leaving his country and his home,
Seeking new sights under eastern skies,
Filled with the youthful desire to roam,
A new world, new life, before him lies,
Eagerly he goes.

But sad and anxious are the hearts he leaves behind,
And many the prayer that is offered for him,
That with each temptation he will find,
The power to resist – that distance will not dim
The trust of those he leaves.
That he will fight life's battles grim,
And come back a man.

Mum was excited to receive news that Dad was on his way home from Egypt. Here are a couple of her writings.

The Day is Here (22nd November, 1945)

So, at last, the day is now here,
    The day you can say you are on your way,
Somehow I cannot believe it dear,
    All the years that have gone seem like a day.

But the last few days that now remain,
    Will be dragging along never ending,
And until I see your face again,
    I pray God your ship is quickly sending.

A Letter to Jim (23rd November, 1945)

Many things I would write,
    But I am not inspired tonight,
I only know I'm missing you,
    And wonder if you miss me too.

And, my darling, I would pray,
    That God has kept you safe today,
That He will bring you quickly home,
    Never from my side to roam.

Mum wrote this the day before her first marriage to Dad.

Gifts

You gave me a jewelled brooch,
You gave me a cross and chain,
You gave me a tender smile,
And kisses in the rain.

Sad to say the brooch I lost,
The cross and chain came apart,
But the smile and the kisses.
Still linger in my heart.

You gave me a diamond ring,
You gave me a promise true,
I gave you my love, sweetheart,
It still belongs to you.

The diamond from our ring has gone,
War has parted you and I,
But my love and your promise,
Are ours until we die.

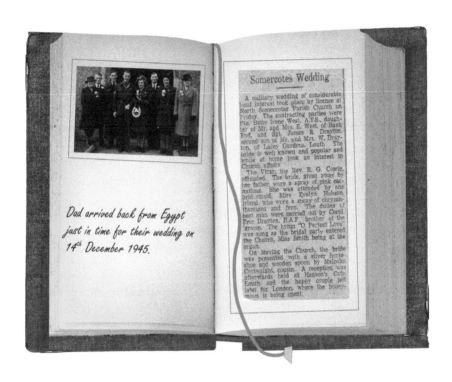

Dad arrived back from Egypt just in time for their wedding on 14ᵗʰ December 1945.

Somercotes Wedding

A military wedding of considerable local interest took place by licence at North Somercotes Parish Church on Friday. The contracting parties were Pte. Bette Irene West, A.T.S., daughter of Mr. and Mrs. E. West, of Bank End, and Sgt. James R. Drayton, second son of Mr. and Mrs. W. Drayton, of Lacey Gardens, Louth. The bride is well known and popular and while at home took an interest in Church affairs.

The Vicar, the Rev. R. G. Cowie, officiated. The bride, given away by her father, wore a spray of pink carnations. She was attended by one bridesmaid, Miss Evelyn Hobson, friend, who wore a spray of chrysanthemums and fern. The duties of best man were carried out by Corpl. Eric Drayton, R.A.F., brother of the bridegroom. The hymn "O Perfect Love" was sung as the bridal party entered the Church, Miss Smith being at the organ.

On leaving the Church, the bride was presented with a silver horseshoe and wooden spoon by Malcolm Cartwright, cousin. A reception was afterwards held at Hanson's Cafe, Louth, and the happy couple left later for London, where the honeymoon is being spent.

Mum was released from her war duties with J Coy Leicester 8/D Group A.T.S. on 12th April, 1946 – by the military dispersal unit York.

Mum and Dad both worked at Louth Canners in the early 1950s. They may have worked there in the later 1940s too but I am not sure of this.

Mum was the editor of Louth Canners' Magazine, although she is referred to as Bette Drayton rather than Betty Drayton. In the 4th edition (Spring 1952) she is now the 'editress' not the 'editor' as in previous editions!

Here is a small selection of her many publications from some of these magazines.

Winter Song

Snowflakes drifting gently down,
On lonely field and busy town.
Covering roofs and furrows slowly,
On palace roof or cottage lowly.
Glittering in the Christmas starlight,
Frost so crisp, and clear, and clean,
The trees with branches all a-gleam.
Purifying earth and air,
For the New Year's crops to bear.
The wind a-whistling round our homes,
Dashing the ocean on sandy domes.
And we may feel our one desire,
To linger round a glowing fire.
Perhaps a little more to rest,
That we may then, with greater zest,
Live the brighter Seasons of another year.

In 1943, Louth Malt Kiln was destroyed by bombing during World War II.

In 1950, a replacement was built. At the time, the concrete building was considered both large and modern. It was the first concrete maltings in Europe.

It was sometimes referred to as the "Concrete Cathedral" and some thought it was a blot on the landscape.

This replacement Malt Kiln was demolished in 2015 to make way for an Aldi supermarket.

The Malt Kiln

Concrete monster, rising daily,
Lording greyly,
Over town.
Unexpectedly on well-known scenes to frown,
Like some great box that's fallen down.
To rest smugly,
Squarely!
Ugly!
From the spire some beauty stealing,
And from Louth that old world feeling.

Good Intentions

On January 1st, nineteen hundred and fifty-one,
My savings, alas, were all but gone,
And I resolved to save.
If I stopped smoking, the position, I thought,
Might not be so grave.
And I realised, as well as that,
That I was getting rather fat,
And though it made the prospect dim,
Most certainly I'd have to slim.
My hair was very far from bright,
So to one hundred strokes per night
I sentenced it.
Into the dentist's I would periodically pop –
Which reminded me, sweets must surely stop.
I would not swear, – no I would NOT!
However bad the crisis got.
And as we draw near fifty-two,
These things I yet resolve to do.
What a splendid person I should be
By nineteen hundred and fifty-three.

Mum didn't stop smoking until the 1970s, was always overweight, she ended up with false teeth in her 50s but I only heard her swear after her stroke in 2000, so I think one of her intentions was achieved!

To a Snowdrop

Such a little humble thing,
But to me what hope you bring,
All the thousand joys of Spring,
And all the joy of living.

Never was a poet born,
Who you could not put to scorn,
Where the writer to express,
In mere words, such hopefulness?

Through the ages you remain,
Heralding the Spring again,
Bringing hope in Winter's gloom,
Ever will the Snowdrop bloom.

She often included reference to snowdrops in her poems!

The Optimist

It seems to me that life must be
Exactly what you make it,
And as we're not here very long,
With a smile and a merry song,
Is the best way to take it.

What's the use of crossing bridges
Before they are in sight,
In getting angry, or in crying,
When you might be trying
To put the wrong things right?

Why spend your days in grieving
For someone who has gone.
They are now beyond all pain.
Why not give your help again
To a needier one?

Why make life such a serious thing,
When it is but a play?
'When a hundred years have gone,
The world will still be going on'.
We shall have had our day!

Why worry about the atom bombs?
There's little we can do.
Why not spread a smile around?
And in a while you will have found
Life is grand for you.

The early 1950s were a significant time of change. Mum and Dad are divorced.

Dad marries my birth mother, Shirley Bates. They have three daughters: Julie (who died in an accident, aged two, in 1955); Carol born in 1954; then me born in 1963.

Mum changes her job and trains to be a shorthand and typist teacher.

Mum also loses her friend, Ray, in February, 1952. She wrote:

The Bequest

To me you leave the memory of a laugh,
Your joy of life:
Although you walked its final path
With unspectacular courage;
Firmly human in every stride.
The memory, for me to treasure,
Of a voice alive with pleasure
To greet me as your friend.
It is all you had to leave me;
And it will last me to the end.

It is June, 1953 and Mum writes about the Coronation of Her Majesty, Queen Elizabeth II. This was published in Louth Canners' Magazine No 9, June, 1953. I believe that this is the last article that she wrote in this publication, before moving on to her new life.

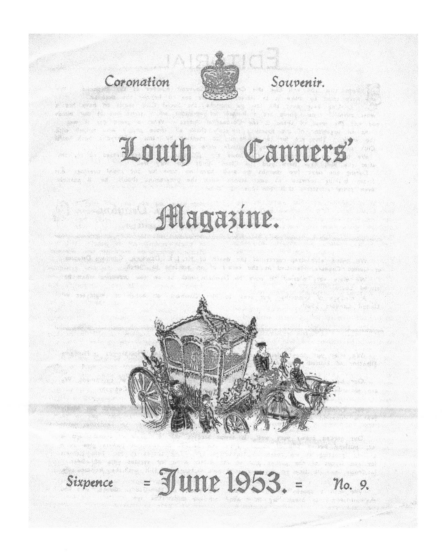

Coronation   Souvenir.

Louth Canners'

Magazine.

Sixpence   = June 1953. =   No. 9.

God save the Queen

"God save the Queen"
   Shout all her people,
Bells in rejoicing ring,
   From church tower and steeple.
God bless Her Majesty,
   So young and so fair;
Endow her with courage,
   Her burden to bear.

"Long may she reign"
   Through glorious years,
In peace and prosperity,
   War far from our fears.
And may this historic land
   Become young in spirit,
By her gracious hand.
   "God save the Queen".

It is sometime in 1954. Mum's life has changed so much. She gives herself some advice and writes 'Live'.

In 2022, selecting her writings for this publication, I feel that I can hear her saying this to me now – as I weep with sorrow and pain, at the loss of my wonderful Mum. How I wish I could take this advice.

Live

My advice to myself, and anyone else
Who will take it, is –
Live, fool live.
Don't you know how short life is?
Never look to the future or the past,
You have only got today!
Cherish it, cling to it.
Take it – pain or joy – it's yours –
All that you have!
All you may ever know.
Take it, and be glad.

In the 1950s, Mum continues to enjoy time in North Somercotes with her brother Stan.

However, on 25th May, 1955 she writes:

Thirty

Today I am thirty;
Alas!
The years – how they pass – how they pass!
In the last of my teens
I could cry at being twenty;
Since then I've shed my tears in plenty,
Until the well is dry.
Disappointment and despair;
Grief and death;
Have become a familiar affair
Which no longer make me cry.
Alas!
The years – how they pass – how they pass!
And leave behind no youthful tears
To heal life's wounds and calm our fears.
I wish that I could cry.

In May, 1956, Mum wrote this under the title 'Woodacres'. It was later published in The Lincolnshire Life County Annual 1966, page 56, under the title MARSHmallows. There is only a slight difference in these two versions, other than the title, the third to last line – in the original version it says, "On the fellside calling". I do not know what prompted her to write this, change it or submit it for publication.

MARSHmallows

We went to the house where we used to live,
    Many years ago;
We travelled the road where we used to walk,
    Where every inch we know
And nothing seemed just quite the same,
    As the memory we had,
The paint, the curtains, all was changed,
    The dear old house looked sad.

We leaned upon the gate a while,
    Looking the meadows over;
Remembering how Daisy and Polly and Bess,
    Came swaying through the clover.
But now there were some unknown cows,
    That munched away unheeding,
And no overtures of ours
    Distracted them from feeding.

The lovely chestnut tree was gone,
    Upon whose ample branches
We'd swarmed and swung, and bruised our knees,
    And taken fearsome chances.
Our little shed had been pulled down,
    Where we would dance and mime,
And all about us we could see
    The changes made by time.

Then a stranger came to the door,
    And in anger glared,
As we leaned on the gate, and looked at her house,
    Resenting us as we stared.
A hostile dog rushed barking madly,
    Children with wide-eyed gaze,
Peered from the window that was ours,
    In those other days.

Sadly then we turned away,
    Our presence was offending,
Where once a welcome glad was ours;
    Where once the days unending,
In carefree hours had gently passed,
    And where in fond protection,
Our lives had seemed so safe and glad,
    So sheltered in affection.

But in our memory the house
    Will always be the same,
As we see the faces of our childhood
    Around us once again;
And hear the happy voices
    Across the marshes calling,
Mingling with the cry of curlews,
    When the night is falling.

I think that Mum may have written this in Autumn in the mid/late 1950s. It was published in Lincolnshire Life Vol 2, No 3, Autumn, 1962 edition, page 49 (poetry corner).

Once again there are snowdrops mentioned in her writings. How she must have loved those flowers and spring!! Every time I see snowdrops they remind me of her.

Autumn

Sadly moans the Autumn breeze,
Into the air there creeps a chill,
And the leaves upon the trees
Blow gold and brave, until –
At last – they fall.
The flowers of the Autumn
Are the brightest and most gay,
Like a condemned man's breakfast
On the execution day.
Oh! The Autumn has it glories,
What artist can deny?
But its golden beauty
Can only make me sigh.
Long dark days are now in store;
How weary I shall be,
Until I see the gentle snowdrop,
Promising lovely Spring to me.

I think that Mum may have written this in the Summer of 1960/1961. It was published in Lincolnshire Life in October, 1962 and The Lincolnshire Life County Annual 1965, page 123. In 1973 she had a different poem published, with the same title but different words.

Harvest Home

The harvest is gathered in,
And we have sung it home,
'Neath humble village chapel roof,
Or great cathedral's mighty dome.

> From Gainsborough to Spalding
> The harvest bells have rung,
> And the voice of our forefathers,
> Seem to join us as we sung.

> Gladly we have garnished
> Ancient pillars with our tithes,
> What matter if the corn was got
> By combine, instead of scythes.

> And around the font we piled
> The riches of the earth,
> As though to show the unborn ones
> What awaits them at their birth.

From the early 1960s I feel that Mum's life is, once again, changing. She starts to get some poems more widely published, as we have seen. In September, 1962 she reflects on her life and writes this.

Why am I always inside the window

Why am I always inside the window,
Looking out,
At the busy world,
As it goes about?
Waiting for my love to come,
Who never comes.
Watching the honey bee,
That round the garden hums.
Why am I always inside the window,
Looking out,
Watching the rain falling down
On the busy people,
As they go rushing off to town?
Not feeling its sting on my face;
Nor basking in the sunshine –
But in the same old place –
Inside the window,
Looking out.

A short time after writing this she decides to make some major changes to her life. She moves to Sheffield and spends time with her extended family. In October 1963, at age 38, she starts her nursing training with The United Sheffield Hospitals, qualifying three years later. I remember her telling me that she often felt like a Mum to the (much younger) other nursing students!

On 31st October, 1967 she, along with other qualified nurses, arrive at St Mary's Hospital Leeds for the one year midwifery course, split into two equal parts. During this time she meets Valerie Clifton, now Valerie Baines, who would become a lifelong friend. In 2022, I am still in touch with her by phone and email.

Here they are, in Leeds on 3rd May, 1968, for a group photo to go in the next day's press as they have now taken their part one exam. Valerie is top row, second from the right and Mum is middle row, third from the right.

Photograph reproduced by kind permission of
The Yorkshire Post and Yorkshire Evening Post.

It is March, 1969. I am five years old. My sister, Carol, is 15. My birth mother, Shirley, has died in an accident. I find this all very confusing; I cannot understand what has happened. Where has she gone? Why has she gone? Did I do something wrong? I can see and hear that Dad and Carol are very upset; often crying. No one can make me understand.

From such sadness, there comes great joy. Months later, my Dad and I meet this lady that I don't know on the promenade at Mablethorpe. Initially, I try to hide behind Dad – maybe she won't see me! However, after a while we are playing on the beach, building sandcastles and she is making me laugh. She is very kind and patient. She smiles a lot. There are many more meetings.

On 1st May, 1970, when I am six years old, this lady – Betty, becomes 'My Mum', when her and Dad marry for a second time. We are so lucky and happy to have her in our life; though, very understandably, to Carol she is not her Mum.

We have a new home. Mum gives up her career as she wants to be a full-time wife and mother. It is not long before Dad's Mum, my 'little nanny', comes to live with us as she cannot cope on her own. Mum's nursing skills come in useful. I remember her getting up at least a couple of times every night to move 'little nanny' in her bed – to stop her getting bed sores. Carol gets married and later on Mum and Dad have a grandson and granddaughter.

This was published in the early 1970s I believe, as Mum has put photos with it – including one of Dad, Mum, me and our inspiring friend, Rosie, who was both deaf and blind; we used to see her at church. There is, of course, her usual reference to snowdrops! Unfortunately, I have not been able to find the publishing details – it was probably Focus, Louth Council of Churches, newsletter.

February

There are snowdrops in the garden, the flowering currant is beginning
to sprout.
Down the canal at Keddington, hazel catkins are coming out.
In Hubbards Hills small signs of life can easily be found.
On marsh and wold the little lambs are skipping all around.
Spring is round the corner and winter's on run.
Soon we'll be at Mablethorpe, lying in the sun.
We'll make castles on the shore
And paddle in the sea once more.
Aren't we trebly blessed in Louth with wold and marsh and sea?
Who wants noisy city life, who wants packaged holiday tours? Not me!

*She would change her mind in the 1980s and early to mid 1990s, about
packaged holiday tours! When Dad was made redundant in 1978, they
went to Holland and then, once Dad retired, they went to several places
on holiday including: Malta, Spain (many times, for a few weeks, in the
winter, Mum hated British winters!), Menorca and Portugal.*

Mum starts to regularly submit poems for publication in Focus – a local church newsletter. I am not sure if these are ones she has already written or what she writes at the time. Here is one that I feel was part of her philosophy of life. Published in Focus, No 15, March, 1973, page 3.

Courage

Courage is the strength that's given, when it seems you cannot win.
The strength to keep soldiering on, and never giving in.
The strength to take a single step, where once you used to run.
To find a calm acceptance. To say, "Thy will be done".
When you cannot find this courage, and let's face the fact, who can?
Most of us are simply human – not some superman.
When you find your own strength failing to fight against the odds,
You must get down on your knees and humbly ask for God's.

In 1956, Mum wrote a poem called 'Ann Peacock', which I believe was never published. She used the first couple of lines and a similar theme, for her published 'May' poem in Focus, No 17, May, 1973, page 2.

May

Little girl, picking daisies, making bracelets and necklaces.
As fresh and pure, as innocent as the meadow is in May.
Your eyes are bright as bluebells. Your hair smells sweet of hay.
Singing, miming, dancing – a princess in your play.
Little girl, store in your heart the memory of this day.
Spring's flowers soon are faded, soon gone the time for play.
Meadows can be split in lots, and swallowed up as building plots.
The golden dust of buttercups the gas bill will not pay.
Too soon you'll learn that diamonds are called a girl's best friend.
The dewy days of lovely May, how quickly they must end.

We spent many happy times at Mablethorpe with family and friends. Here is one that was published in Focus, No 20, August, 1973, page 2.

Holidays

Thank God for all the happy days we spend beside the sea.
For space of sand, for flowing tide, making us gay and free.
We cannot wait to shed our clothes,
Feel the surge of ocean through our toes.
Tingling, taunting every vein.
Tang of spray on our lips again.

Marvellous the things we find
That other tides have left behind.
Star fishes, timber and sea snails,
Fragile shells, like babies' finger nails.
We laze amongst the marram grasses
That whisper as the warm breeze passes.

Feel the silky, sunbaked sand,
Beneath our tanned and languid hand.
"Thank God – Thank God" cry the seagulls, as on silver wings they fly.
Joyously spiralling, poising, against the August sky.

It is early 2022 as I read, and reread, Mum's poems and writings; carefully deciding which to include in this publication. The current news headlines are full of increasing fuel and food costs. There is war in Ukraine. Times are very worrying. I came across this poem, initially attracted to it because of its title, and it certainly made me think. I am unsure when it was written but it was published in Focus, No 27, March, 1974, page 2.

The cost of living

The cost of living's always high for those who seek this way to tread.
Who taught us, that to live life fully, we need more than bread.
Who gave us rules concerned with sharing and with caring.
Who, tempted, scorned all worldly powers.
Who pointed to the wayside flowers
And said "Why do you worry so –
See these lillies, how they grow".
The cost of life is in the living,
In the loving and the giving.
In caring for our neighbour,
As our Lord commanded,
A Christian life is costly,
Of all we have demanding.
But the reward is the gift of peace,
"Which passeth understanding".

It is 1974. Mum's parents, my Nanny and Grandad West, are celebrating their Golden Wedding. Money is very tight so there is no big party, just a few close family round to our house. Mum loved to cook and bake whenever she could; so, of course, she made their lovely Golden Wedding Cake. As well as making the cake, she wrote about it too. Published in Focus, No 32, August, 1974, page 2.

Golden Wedding Cake

Ingredients for the Golden Wedding Cake on the kitchen table stand.
What memories each bring to me, as they come to hand.
The childhood years when, tip-toes, we tried to see,
What treat was being made and we had to – "Wait till tea".

Wartime years, rations saved for months for celebrations.
Picnics and parties, happy faces of old friends and long-passed loved
relations.
The cherries bring to me the smiles, the almonds bring the tears.
The recipe of family life over fifty years.

All mixed up together, folded in with love, to make
A cake that's truly golden – this Golden Wedding Cake.

*It was a couple of years later when Nanny died. Always so very caring,
Mum spent a lot of her time looking after Grandad, until his death in
1987.*

Published in Focus, No 35, November, 1974, page 2.

The Unknown Soldier

They say we should forget him now, the lad who died at Mons.
Especially now we're Europeans and our nationalism gone.
We read late General's memoirs and hear the Statemen's musing
Of how, in retrospective light, he was but a pawn for using.

Yet – how often do I feel him near, this lad with cheerful grin.
Not only in November days, with dark nights drawing in.
But in a lane in springtime when birds are chirruping.
On a crowded beach in summer, where my grandson plays with sand.
Sometimes behind a family group I think I see him stand.

He died for what he thought was right. That is the simple fact.
No complicated thesis from such courage can detract.
Silence may be shattered; poppies no longer worn.
I can't forget – though it happened all those years ago – I wasn't even
born!

*Tragically the grandson she refers to in this poem, Stephen Paul Cliffe,
died in an accident on 17th August, 1993, aged just 21.*

Mum often wrote about seasons or months. Here is one about September. Published in Focus, No 33, September, 1974, page 8.

September

September! How can it be?
Where has the year gone, why so speedily?
So recently we waited the coming of the spring
And already silvery autumn mists across the meadows cling.

In life's September how we note the relentless hours pass.
Why – it's not five minutes since we jumped the stiles and ran and skipped to class.
So short a time since we could dance our springtime nights away.
Now the sight of children's energy makes us weary, as they play.

What have we done with all that time?
What have we got to show?
As you change the calendar,
Do you wonder where time goes?

Both Mum and her brother, Stan, loved birds. This was published in Focus, No 42, June, 1975, page 2.

Birds

Of all God's creatures, if I weren't me, what do you think I'd like to be? – A bird!

Almost with envy I watch them flying, floating, swooping, swimming, diving, true masters of the sea and air.

They build their homes with artistry, each according to his needs, high up in the tree tops or down among the reeds.

In utterly unjoyful weather I have seen them shrug their feathers and sing. There's not a Mozart or a Callas can teach a blackbird anything.

What lessons they've taught, what joy they've brought to us since time began. I watch admiring this awe-inspiring, gladsome companion.

It is the summer of 1975. We are once again on the beach at Mablethorpe. Spending time with Mum and Dad's grandchildren. Mum is now 50 and feeling her age, as she writes 'To The Young'. Published in Focus, No 44, August, 1975, page 2.

To The Young

I watch you skip and dance and run,
On the seashore having fun.
Swift legs, strong arms, all brown, still growing.
Eyes, oh – brighter than any summer sun –
With health and merriment are glowing.

Immobile, overweight, limbs aching in unaccustomed heat.
Swelling round the ankles, "Oh – my poor feet!".
That's me.

How little time ago, upon these very sands,
I played, as you are doing now, there standing on your hands.
Sea breezes tangling through your hair.
Laughing, singing, not a care.

Middle-age! Who wants to know?
Enjoy each precious minute – for it will be so.

This was published in Focus, No 45, September, 1975, page 2. I am not sure what prompted her to write this!

Compromise

How often do we meet some situation,
Which threatens to drive us mad with anger or frustration?
Although we try with all our might,
It seems that nothing will go right.
"What's the use of trying", we mutter and we grumble.
Does the Lord send difficult times to teach us to be humble?
To give us sympathy with others when they are similarly troubled?
To remind us we're only human and however grand the plan,
We often have to compromise and do the best we can.

Mum would often write about times of the year; here are some about Christmas, Easter and the New Year. With her strong Christian faith, religious times of the year were very important to Mum.

Published in Focus, No 48, December, 1975, page 2.

Christmas Grace

Lord, as we sit down in this festive place, surrounded by your plentitude; loving smiles on every face, that make Christmas candlelight superfluous; let us not be unmindful of those who go unsheltered, who, in December storm, have not so much as stable-room, or ox to keep them warm.

Lord, give to the unloved, the lonely and afraid, the gift you came to bring. The hope that transcends misery, that cancels out man's sin. The hope that shines throughout the world with sure and certain glow. The hope you brought at Bethlehem, those many years ago.

Published in Focus, No 60, December, 1976, page 2.

Bells of Bethlehem

"Peace on earth, goodwill to men ….", ring out the bells of Bethlehem.
Christ is born this very day, come to earth with men to stay!
A liberating Lord He comes; with love He rules, not tanks and guns.
One day all men will understand and live in peace, as He commands.

Bells of Bethlehem, sweet and clear;
Christ is born again this year.
Not long ago, in an old forgotten time –
But here and now – He comes to us in twentieth century bread and wine.

New Year's Eve

Bells of St James' ring out the old in the new and we are momentarily suspended,
Between the year that is to come and the one now ended.

In one short holding of the breath, between adjacent years,
A flash of passing joys and sorrows, of future hopes and fears.
Awareness of time's slipping, ungraspable, through our fingers,
But 1975 has gone, we're not allowed to linger.

Impatiently the young folk wait to burst balloons and cheer,
Rashly wishing time away, eager for another year.
Older folk, how well they know that the years, which once seemed plenty,
Speed by at an alarming pace, after reaching twenty.

The New Year

Here then is another year, with paths untrodden, new,
Leading out into the future – a gift from God to you.
A chance to take another road, if the way you've walked seems wrong,
To take courage in your kitbag, to try walking with a song.
A chance to turn and think again – a chance to make amends.
A chance to try out new ideas, perhaps to make new friends.
But hurry! Hurry! Don't delay, for time is quickly flying.
Chances get missed, hopes go astray, the year is already dying.

Easter Anthem

April comes and Resurrection. Sing out anthems loud and clear.
Mankind – stop your mournful march and hear!
Now is the time of great renewing, when larks and linnets shout.
STOP! LOOK! LISTEN! – busy people – See the daffodils are out!

Can't you hear their golden trumpets Easter's certainty declare?
There's sorrowing and suffering, most folks get their share.
But Easter gives us courage to fight against despair.
A hope in life's confusion. A purpose in all pain.

> Christ has died.
> Christ has risen.
> Christ will come again.

Published in Focus, No 16, April, 1973, page 2.

Easter Morning

Easter anthems upward raising.
The risen Christ we are praising.
Easter lillies' heavy perfume drifting over altar rails.
Gone Good Friday, the cross – the nails.
In the morning garden, strangely tranquil,
Blooms the daffodil and jonquil.

Everywhere Spring's tender flowers tell us that the year's dark hours,
too, have gone.
Each blade, each twig, it seems, proclaim that Christ is risen, is risen
again.
Yet, as we wonder at the glory, at the beauty all around us now,
Do we think we hear The Gardener gently ask, "Whom seekest thou?".

I am not sure when Mum wrote this 'Thank You for Mothers' but it has been sung on several Mothering Sundays, at St James' Church in Louth, to the tune 'Morning Has Broken'.

It has been referred to as the 'Gradual Hymn at St James''

Father in Heaven,
Thank you for mothers,
Loving and caring
All the day long;
Thank you for fathers,
Working to feed us
Mothers and fathers
Loving and strong.

Thank you for Mary,
'Blest among women',
She who was chosen
To mother your Son;
Pattern of goodness,
Trust and obedience,
Help us to love you
As she has done.

Loving and caring,
The Church is our Mother;
Telling of Jesus,
Telling of grace,
Filled with his Spirit,
Making us brothers,
Joining his people
In every place.

By contrast, here is one that I feel would definitely not be said/sung in church! Published in Focus, No 51, March, 1976, page 2.

For Mothering Sunday

Mothers don't come like they used to these days,
All smelling of violets and smothered in lace,
With sweet, gentle voices and feminine grace,
As we are led to believe they once did!

Most mothers came in a bustle and stew,
Sharp-tongued and short-tempered, with two jobs to do.
Wearing Dad's jeans and driving their car.
In the last fifty years Mum's travelled far.

Yet, unchanged by time, the concern and the care,
The old-fashioned love in her eyes is still there.
Whether you're five or fifty-three
I am sure you will agree.
There's no-one just like Mum for me!

How very true Mum.

Snowdrops again!! Published in Focus, No 50, February, 1976, page 2.

Snowdrop

When it seems that Spring will never come and winter never pass,
This humble flower speaks of hope, its freshness sparkling like a star,
in the muddy, jaded grass.

In dark and shady places, there the snowdrop grows,
Clustering underneath the trees, modest, unassuming, in character
how different from flamboyant summer rose.

Does it remind you of someone you know, who, when times are hard,
in a quiet, gentle way,
Can act with tact and sympathy, knows just the word to say?
Who gives hope and reassurance that unhappiness will pass away,
As surely as the snowdrop does upon a winter day.

Mum continues to publish something for most months in 1976. I will not include them all, but I feel that this one definitely needs including – she would often say it! She often thought it and she often wrote about the importance of today. It was part of her philosophy of life. Published in Focus, No 54, June, 1976, page 2.

Do it now!

Do it now – don't wait – or you'll find it is too late.

Too late to speak the words of cheer, loving words, words of comfort, someone waits to hear.

Too late to speak the words of praise, that make someone's life much brighter, to offer out a helping hand and make the load seem lighter.

Too late to give the gift you planned, to show, with loving touch of hand, how much you care, that you forgive and understand.

Do it now – don't wait! Tomorrow never never comes and it always is too late.

This was published in Focus, No 57, September, 1976, page 2. The St Mary's Cemetery that she refers to is the one in Louth, off the Grimsby Road.

Honesty

A purse, put down so carelessly, on a bench, beneath a tree, in St Mary's Cemetery.

Well, you know how it is, I'm sure,
As prices go up more and more!
How easy to divert a while, on a lovely summer day.
To linger near those age-old trees, get carried far away.
To ponder on the lives of those townsfolk, whose stones, against the wall,
Stand, a green and crumbling regiment. With ivy fast encroaching to annihilate them all.

Here, one cannot fail to marvel at, and, once again, admire,
The perfection of St James', symmetry of pinnacles, slenderness of spire.
Rising with a gracefulness, to the eye, well-pleasing.
How many centuries will it stand, to offer praise unceasing?

The hour strikes my consciousness, with deep, unhurried pace,
Reminding me to hurry home. There's the usual jobs to face.

And my purse, left there so carelessly?
It was home as soon as me!
We hear of a world of greed and hate,
But honesty's not dead, in Louth, at any rate!

If you recall Mum wrote a poem called 'God save the Queen', which was published in Louth Canners' Magazine No 9, June, 1953. She adapted this poem for this 'Jubilee' one – which was published in Focus, No 66, June, 1977, page 2.

Jubilee

"God save the Queen",
Shout all her peoples.
Bells, in rejoicing, ring,
From church towers and steeples.
Long live Her Majesty,
Who, for twenty-five years,
Has served her people steadfastly,
Has shared our hopes and fears,
Who, to our ancient monarchy
Has brought the modern touch.
Human, caring,
Elizabeth, God bless you.
We love you very much!

In the late 1970s and 1980s, when the parish of Louth were short of clergy, many lay teams were formed – Mum and Dad were part of this and took many services including evensong, on various occasions, in St James' Church. I think Mum might have been too busy to write much for publication at this time as I am unable to locate many. She was probably preparing for the services that they took. Dad retired in 1988 and they enjoyed many holidays, both abroad and in the UK.

One especially memorable holiday was when Mum, Dad, Trev and I went to Canada in September 1989. We went to Toronto, Niagara Falls and Ottawa. Whilst in Ottawa, we stayed with Mum's midwifery friend, Val, her husband John and their family. Mum was overjoyed to see Val again. They would write to each other often, but that is not the same as seeing each other. Val and John also came to see Mum and Dad at their home on 4th August, 2000.

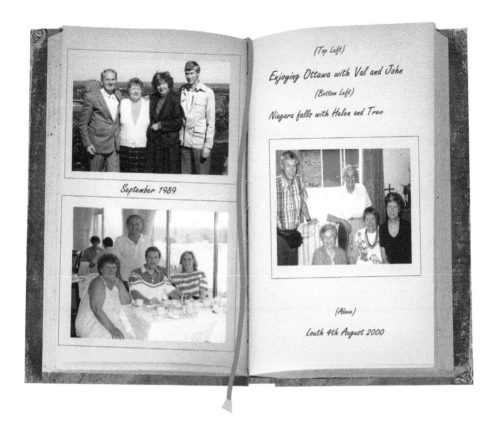

September 1989

(Top Left)

Enjoying Ottawa with Val and John

(Bottom Left)

Niagara falls with Helen and Trev

(Above)

Louth 4th August 2000

Mum writes 'The Library' on 18ᵗʰ August, 1998. I believe that it was never published as I have only found a handwritten version. She is thinking about the end of her life.

At 73, she was struggling with ill health and often needed a wheelchair when we went out, but this didn't stop her enjoying life as much as possible. In September, 1998 Mum, Dad, Trev and I went to Coronation Street, as this was one of the things that she wanted to do. A couple of years after this was when Mum had her stroke and it left her with significant disabilities.

The Library

Seventy years ago I came into a library called "Life".
Books stretched out upon the shelves in endless seeming file.
How I clasped and read them – the books called Baby Play;
Childhood; Schooldays; Adolescence; Womanhood; – they all came
my way.

Some books were full of sweetness, that I remember yet.
Loving words and kind deeds I never will forget.
But then there were the sad ones, with tears on every leaf.
Painfully distressing, full of aching grief.

Now I see in front of me in letters large and bold,
A door marked as the EXIT, into a world unknown.
Will all that world be sweetness? Will there be no pain?
Will I see those loved ones smile at me again?

So I wait within the queue,
To leave the books behind,
Pass through the door and go
Elsewhere, like the rest of humankind.

This needs no explanation from me – it is all here in Mum's words. Taken from The Louth Herald, October, 2002, page 13.

Stillness

Who was it who said, in recent times, "Be careful for what you pray. Your prayer might be answered"? Jesus was in no doubt about it, saying, "Ask and it shall be given unto you".

In 1982 I wrote the following words for a hymn. It was a great pleasure for me when the organist played the piano, which was then near the pulpit in St James', for a joint service of the three Louth branches of the Mothers' Union in May, and we sang these words to the tune, "Now the day is over".

> Lord, grant us time for stillness,
> A time to rest in faith,
> A time to know Your presence,
> Enfolding us always.
>
> A time to be ensheltered,
> Safe in those loving arms,
> Though daily cares press round us,
> And all the world's alarms.
>
> A time to hear You speaking,
> For listening to Your will,
> In humble, quiet obedience,
> Our noisy clamour still.
>
> A time for being empty,
> All sin and shame cast out,
> When peace and love and healing,
> Replace the fear and doubt.
>
> A quietness of being,
> When time itself stands still,
> And glimpses of the eternal,
> Our inward vision fill.

Since being incapacitated by a stroke, two years ago, I have had plenty of time for stillness, and am so grateful for the prayers of Christians in Louth which continue to give me time to rest in faith.

Betty Drayton

In January, 1975 Mum wrote 'A Prayer for 1975', which was published in Focus, No 37, January, 1975, page 2. She adapted this slightly for 2003 and this was published in The Louth Herald, January, 2003, page 13.

A Prayer for 2003

Lord, we pray in 2003 for a greater joy in living,
For awareness that fulfilment comes through loving and through giving.
Whatever be our limitations,
As individuals, or as nations,
We can all do something, we can do our share
In easing someone's burdens, in lightening someone's care.
There's always someone, somewhere, who needs a helping hand,
Or just someone to listen, to try to understand.
If we could make our resolution "to give" and not "to get",
This could be the happiest year the world has known as yet.

This may have been the last thing that Mum wrote as she sadly passed away on 9th February, 2003.

However, in The Louth Herald of February 2003 there was a full A4 page article about Sunday School party (c1930's) which she wrote. Also, in this publication dated May, 2003, there was a lengthy article she wrote about the Blessings of May, so maybe these were written after the adapted prayer above? Neither Dad nor I submitted these in her name after her death. It is a mystery.

She is buried in her beloved North Somercotes, as she wished, not far from where she was born.

My Dad sadly passed away on 15th September, 2021 and they are now reunited, as they both wished.

To My Mum

Thank you, for loving Dad for most of your life,

For agreeing, a second time, to become his wife.

Thank you, for choosing to be My Mum,

For showing me the good life still to come.

Thank you, for being so loving and caring,

For instilling in me the importance of sharing.

Thank you, for the laughter and joy,

For saying you were glad I wasn't a boy!

Thank you, for making me feel I belong,

For teaching me right from wrong.

Thank you, for helping me to be tough,

For supporting me through times that were rough.

Thank you, for the unconditional love that you gave,

For I feel this still, from beyond your grave.

Thank you, for being You, My Mum.

Helen

Lightning Source UK Ltd.
Milton Keynes UK
UKHW050758130922
408768UK00006B/280